A BOOK OF STARS FOR YOU

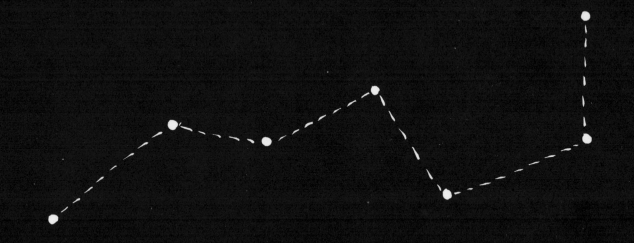

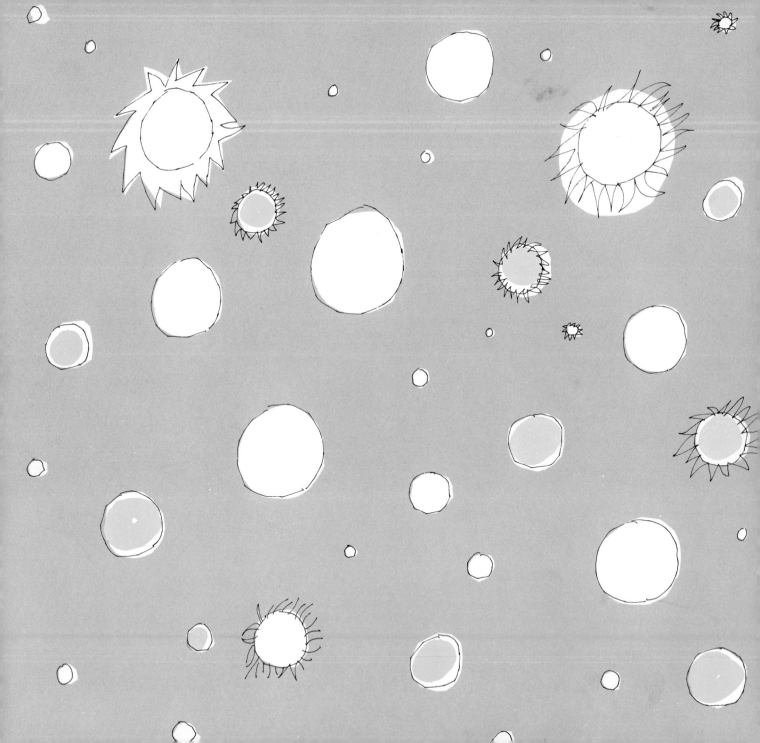

A BOOK OF
STARS
FOR YOU

By Franklyn M. Branley

Illustrated by Leonard Kessler

1967

Thomas Y. Crowell Company   New York

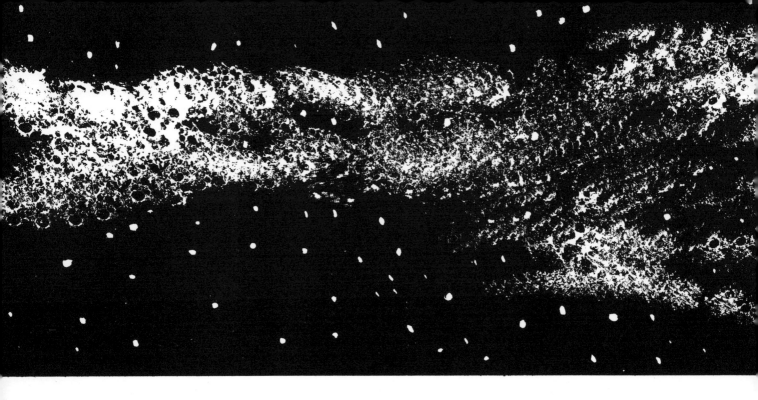

Manufactured in the United States of America

L.C. Card 67-18509

4   5   6   7   8   9   10

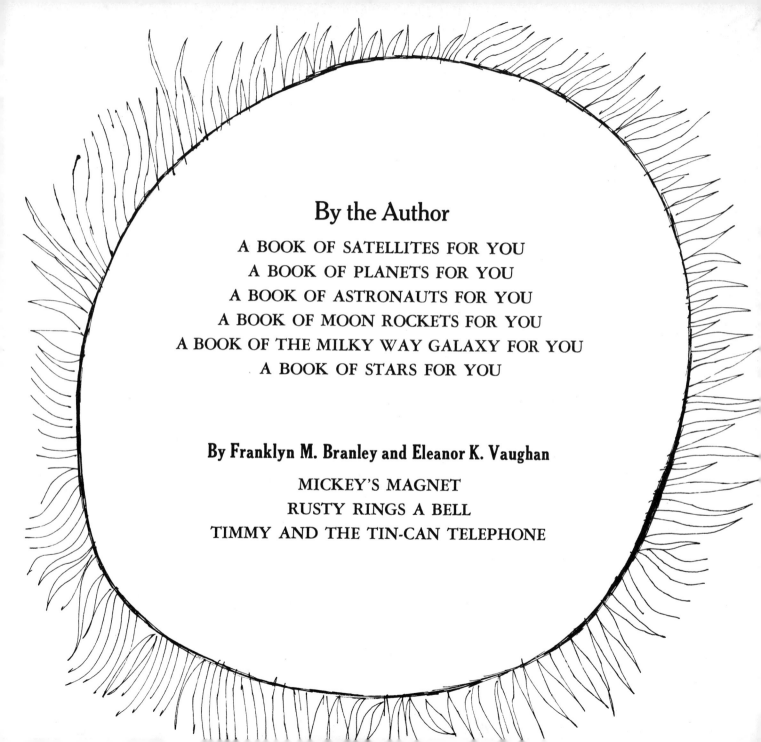

By the Author

A BOOK OF SATELLITES FOR YOU
A BOOK OF PLANETS FOR YOU
A BOOK OF ASTRONAUTS FOR YOU
A BOOK OF MOON ROCKETS FOR YOU
A BOOK OF THE MILKY WAY GALAXY FOR YOU
A BOOK OF STARS FOR YOU

By Franklyn M. Branley and Eleanor K. Vaughan

MICKEY'S MAGNET
RUSTY RINGS A BELL
TIMMY AND THE TIN-CAN TELEPHONE

If someone asked you how many stars you could see on a clear, dark night, what would you answer? Would you say ten thousand, a hundred thousand? Some people think they can see millions of stars—more than you could ever count. But they are wrong. It would be hard to count the stars, but it can be done. If you counted them you would be surprised at how few you can see. You would be lucky if at one time you could count fifteen hundred stars.

At the ocean, on the desert, or high on a mountaintop, where there is little dust in the air and no lights of cities and towns, you can see more stars. Here you can see the dim ones and also the bright ones. In such places you could count almost five thousand stars.

If you looked at the sky through strong binoculars or a small telescope you would see millions of stars. Then you would see more than you could count.

Yet even with a big telescope you see only a small part of all the stars. Astronomers who use the largest telescopes still cannot see them all. They can see only a few billion.

The stars they see belong to a family of stars, gases, and planets called the Milky Way Galaxy. In this galaxy there are many

more stars than we can see. Astronomers believe there are at least 100 billion stars. If you wrote out that number you would have a one followed by eleven zeros—100,000,-000,000. If you counted one star a second, it would take you more than thirty thousand years to count 100 billion. All these stars are in the Milky Way Galaxy.

The earth is one of the nine planets that go around the sun. The sun and the planets, the moon and the satellites of the other planets, the comets, asteroids, and meteoroids make up the solar system. The solar system is located in the Milky Way Galaxy.

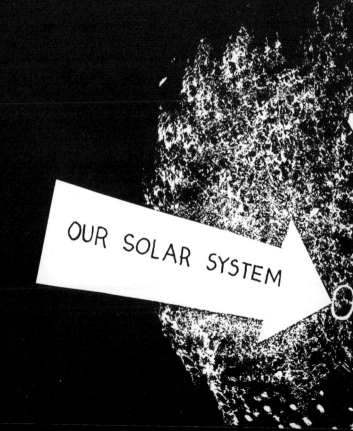

OUR SOLAR SYSTEM

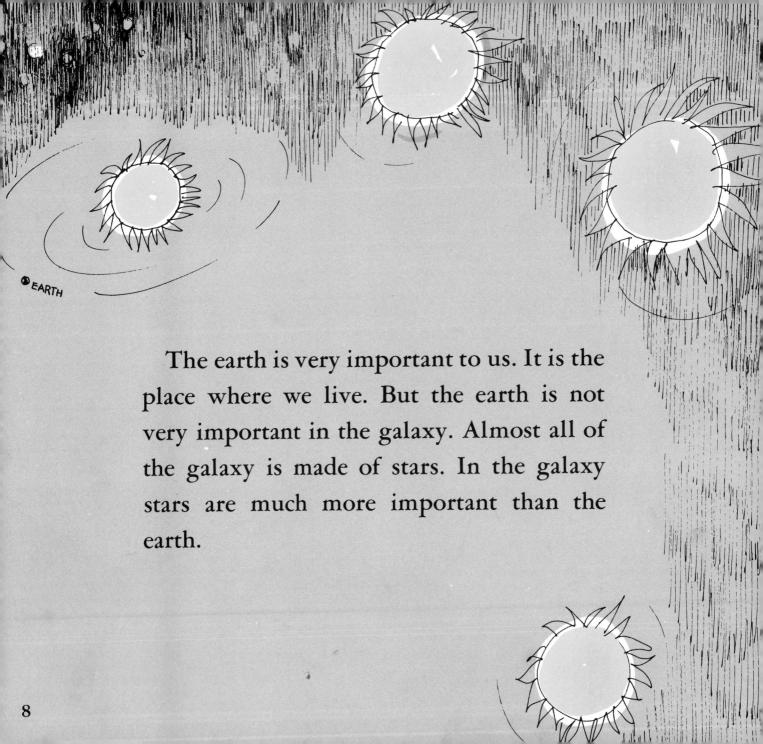

The earth is very important to us. It is the place where we live. But the earth is not very important in the galaxy. Almost all of the galaxy is made of stars. In the galaxy stars are much more important than the earth.

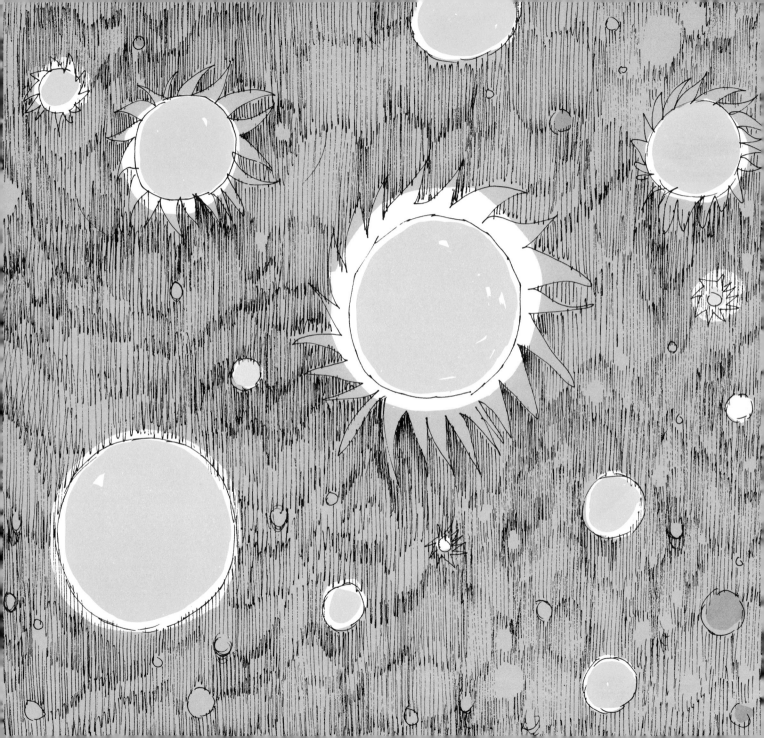

In addition to the stars there are gases in the galaxy that may become stars after a long time. These gases, together with the stars, add up to almost all the material in the galaxy. But there is a little bit left over. All the planets that we know about are made of this little bit of extra material.

Our galaxy is only one of billions of galaxies in the universe. And every galaxy contains billions of stars. So let's find out what stars are, where they come from, and how long they last.

The sun is a star. It is the one that is nearest to the earth, and the star we know most about.

Even though it is the nearest star, the sun is a long way from earth. If you were to travel to the sun in a space ship, going 25,000 miles an hour, it would take you five months to get there. You would have to travel about 93 million miles to reach the sun.

FIVE MONTHS TO TRAVEL TO THE SUN

100,000 YEARS TO TRAVEL TO ALPHA CENTAURI

All the other stars are much farther away from earth than the sun. They are so far away that they look like small points of light, even through big telescopes. After the sun, the next nearest star to earth (Alpha Centauri) is about 26 trillion (26,000,000,-000,000) miles away. If you traveled 25,000 miles an hour, it would take more than 100,000 years to reach Alpha Centauri.

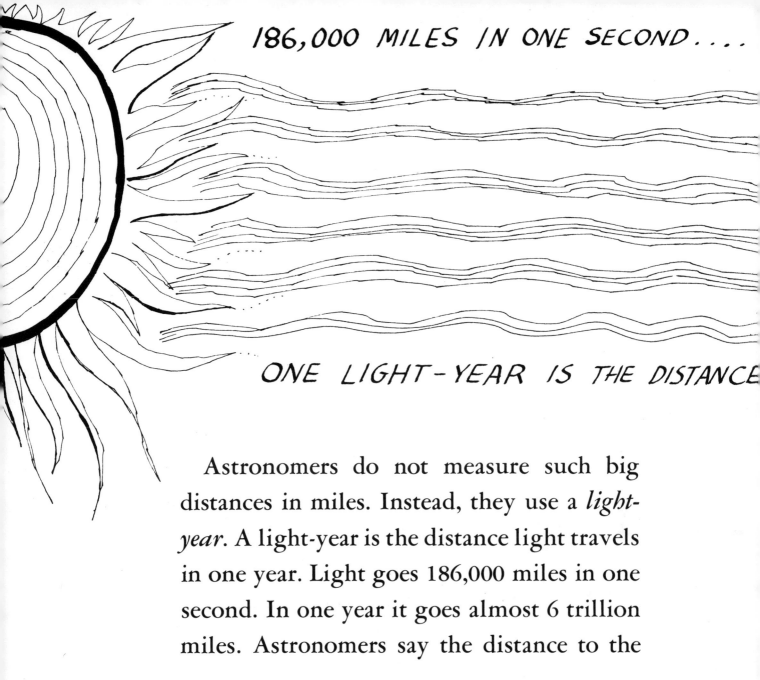

186,000 MILES IN ONE SECOND....

ONE LIGHT-YEAR IS THE DISTANCE

Astronomers do not measure such big distances in miles. Instead, they use a *light-year*. A light-year is the distance light travels in one year. Light goes 186,000 miles in one second. In one year it goes almost 6 trillion miles. Astronomers say the distance to the

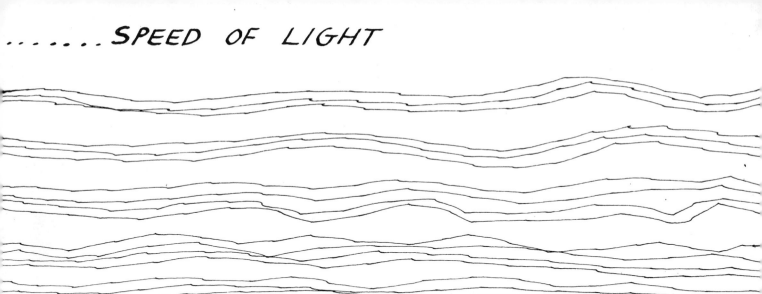

THAT LIGHT TRAVELS IN ONE YEAR

sun—93 million miles—is 8½ light-minutes. It takes light that long to travel from the sun to the earth. Astronomers say the distance to Alpha Centauri is 4⅓ light-years. It takes that long for light to travel from Alpha Centauri to the earth.

When we look at the stars they all seem to be the same distance away. The stars appear to be on a flat surface. But they are not. When we look at the group of stars that make up Orion, which is often called the Hunter or the Giant, they look like this.

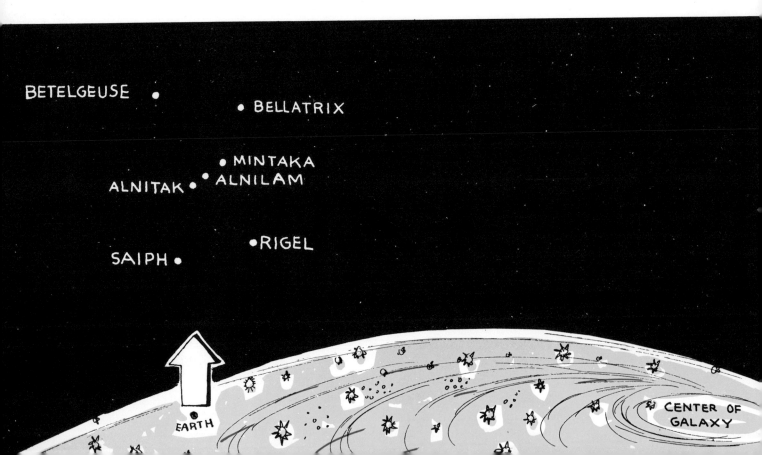

That's because we are at the position in the galaxy shown in the drawing and each star seems to be the same distance from us. When we look at Orion, we look in the direction shown by the arrow.

If we could move to another location in the galaxy, and look at the same stars, we would not see the Hunter at all. We would see that some of the stars in Orion are farther away from earth than others. The stars would look like this.

BETELGEUSE

BELLATRIX

MINTAKA
ALNILAM

ALNITAK

SAIPH

RIGEL

EARTH   IF WE MOVED TO ANOTHER POSITION

When you look at the sky on a clear night the stars seem close together. But they are millions upon millions of miles apart. Here are the main stars in Orion. The three belt stars seem to be close together. But the distance between Alnitak and Alnilam and between Alnilam and Mintaka is billions of miles.

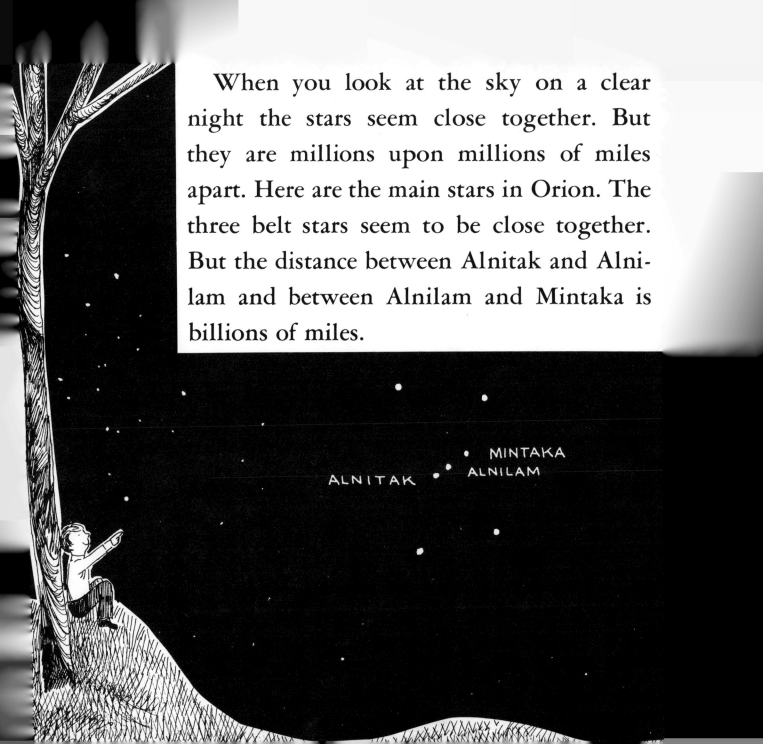

MINTAKA

ALNILAM

ALNITAK

Because stars are very far away, they appear quite different from the way they really are. Each star appears single. But many stars are two stars moving around each other. Some stars that appear to be one are really three, four, five, or even more stars that move around one another. We see every star, whether it is single, double, triple, or more, as a small point of light. Some stars are brighter than others, but each one appears to be the same size. All except the sun.

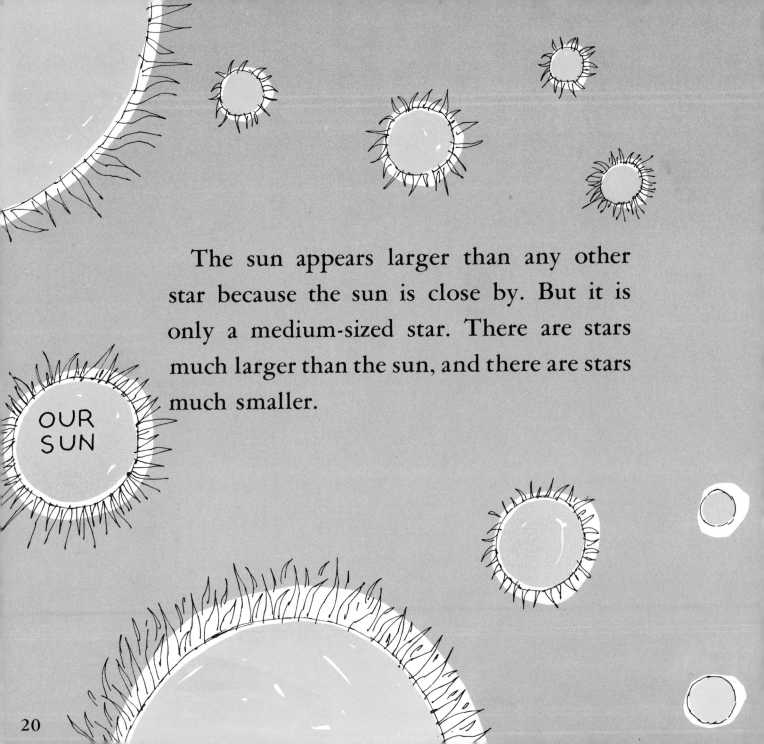

The sun appears larger than any other star because the sun is close by. But it is only a medium-sized star. There are stars much larger than the sun, and there are stars much smaller.

OUR SUN

864,000 MILES

The diameter of the sun, the distance across and through the center, is 864,000 miles. That's just a bit less than one million miles. If the sun were a big hollow ball, over a million earths could be put inside of it.

Betelgeuse, a red star in Orion, is almost 500 million miles in diameter. We call it a red supergiant star. Mercury, Venus, earth, and Mars are the four planets closest to the sun. Betelgeuse is so big that if it were the center of the solar system, it would extend beyond Mars.

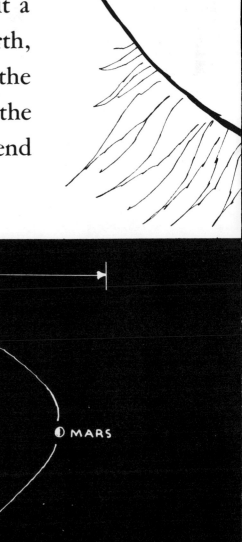

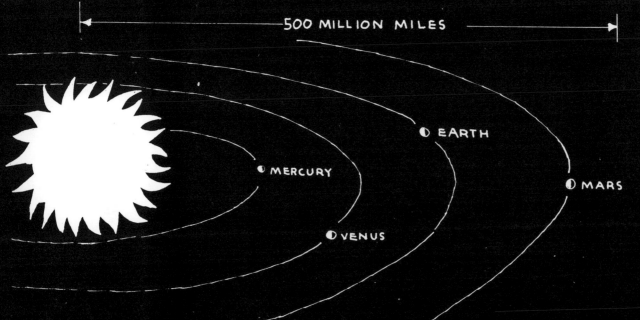

500 MILLION MILES

MERCURY

EARTH

VENUS

MARS

Betelgeuse is not the biggest of all the stars. Two of the biggest stars astronomers know about are Epsilon Aurigae, which has a diameter of about one billion miles, and VV Cephei, which has a diameter of almost two billion miles.

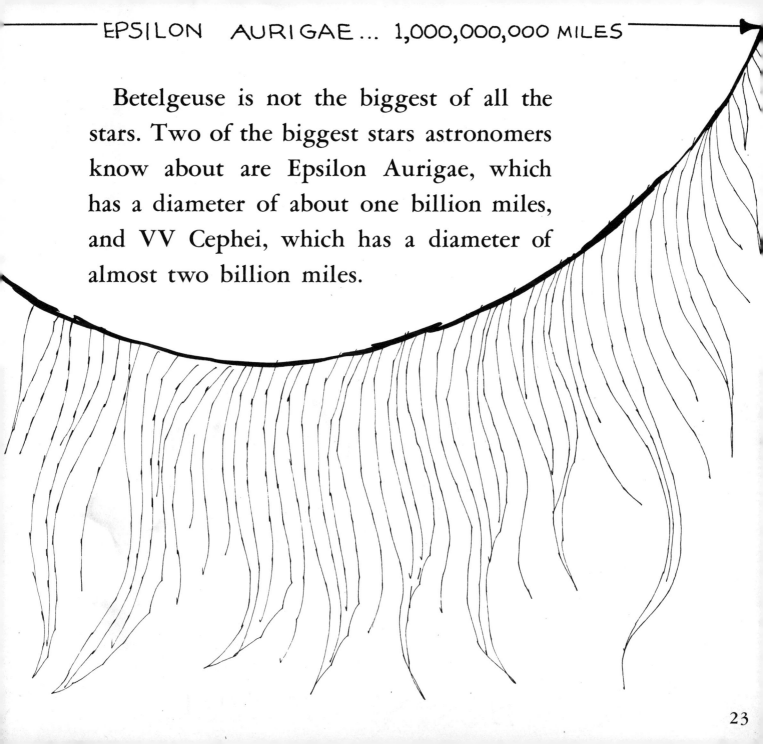

23

Small stars are called dwarf stars. The first one to be discovered is a star that goes around Sirius once in fifty years. We cannot see the star but we know it is there because it affects Sirius. It causes Sirius to move from side to side. It has a diameter of about 29,000 miles. The diameter of the earth is about 8,000 miles.

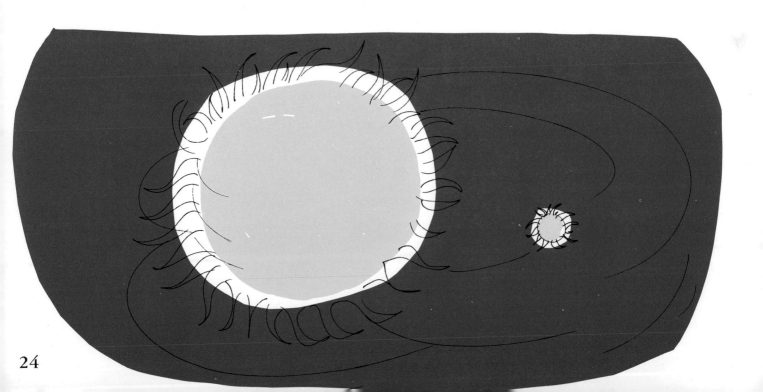

OUR MOON

LP 768-500

But there are stars in our galaxy that are much smaller than the companion of Sirius. One called Van Maanen's Star has a diameter of only 6,000 miles. The smallest star we know of has no name. It is given the number LP768-500. Its diameter is only about 1,000 miles. That is less than one half the diameter of the moon.

Stars vary a great deal in size, but the amount of material they contain does not vary as much.

The sun is big enough to contain more than a million earths. But all the matter in the sun adds up to only about 330,000 earths. That means the matter in most of the sun—the outer part especially—is not packed together as tightly as it is in the earth. It is spread out much more thinly than the material in the earth. We say the density of the sun is less than the density of the earth.

Here is a way to understand what density is. Suppose there are thirty children in your classroom. If there were sixty children, the density in the room would be twice as high. If there were only fifteen children, the density would be half as much.

30 CHILDREN

60 CHILDREN

15 CHILDREN

There are stars that have a density much less than the density of the sun. In the very big stars like Betelgeuse and VV Cephei the density is so low (the gases are spread out so thinly) that you could go right through them without even knowing it.

The density of the air we breathe is three thousand times greater than the density of supergiant stars.

All stars contain a great deal of material, thousands of times more than the earth contains. In big stars the material is spread out. In small stars it is packed together tightly. The density is high. The gases in such stars are packed so tightly that one pint would weigh about 190 tons.

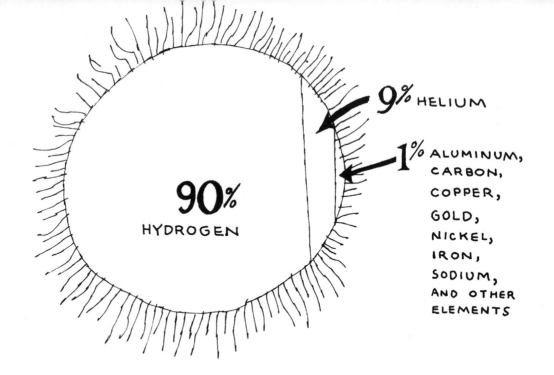

90%
HYDROGEN

9% HELIUM

1% ALUMINUM, CARBON, COPPER, GOLD, NICKEL, IRON, SODIUM, AND OTHER ELEMENTS

Stars are made of the same elements that we have here on the earth: iron, oxygen, hydrogen, sodium, gold, and so on. About 90 percent of the sun is the gas called hydrogen, and almost 10 percent of it is helium, another gas. Aluminum, carbon, copper, gold, nickel, iron, sodium, and scores of other elements make up the other 1 percent of the sun.

All the materials in the sun are in the form of gases. Indeed, all stars are made of gases. Sometimes the gases have little more substance than a shadow; sometimes they are dense as deep inside the sun. In some stars they are so dense that a small volume would weigh many tons.

The gases in stars are very hot, also. Your temperature is 98.6 degrees. The temperature of a hot oven is 500 degrees; iron melts at 3,000 degrees. At the surface of very hot stars the temperature is 50,000 degrees or more.

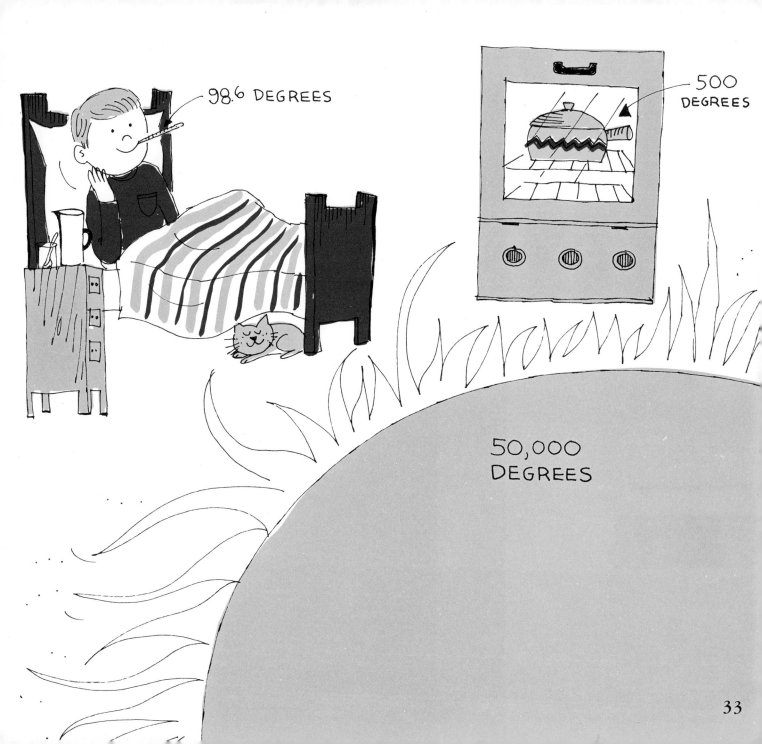

98.6 DEGREES

500 DEGREES

50,000 DEGREES

Very hot stars are blue in color, or bluish white. Cool stars have surface temperatures of 3,000 degrees or lower. These stars are dull red in color. At the surface of the sun the temperature is about 10,000 degrees. It is a yellow-orange star. We say that the sun is a medium-hot star.

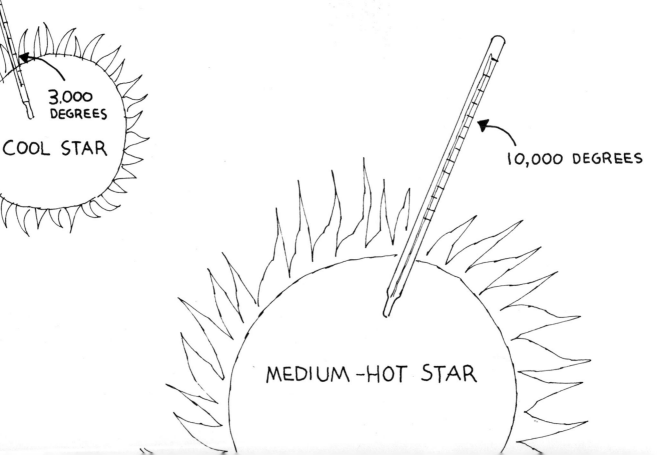

3,000 DEGREES

COOL STAR

10,000 DEGREES

MEDIUM-HOT STAR

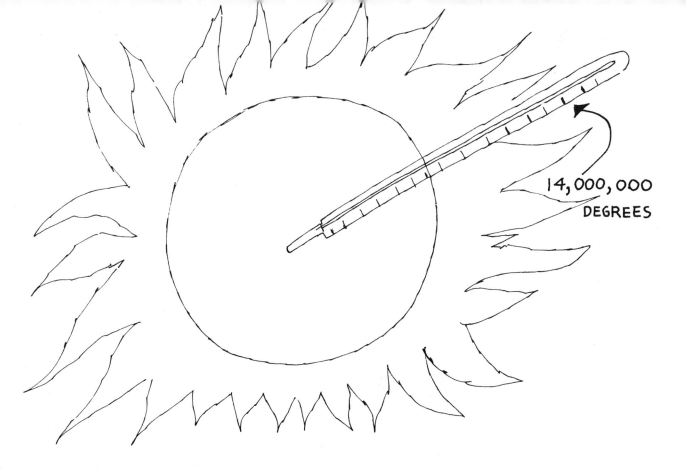

14,000,000 DEGREES

Inside stars the temperature is much higher than it is on the outside. Astronomers have never been able to measure the temperature at the center of the sun, of course. But they can figure out the temperature. They think it must be about 14 million degrees.

The heat and light that keep you alive come from the sun. All through the year the sun acts like a furnace producing heat to warm the whole world. In winter a furnace in your home produces the heat that keeps you warm. A furnace burns coal, oil, or some other fuel. In the sun there is no coal or oil: there is no burning. What keeps the sun and other stars so hot?

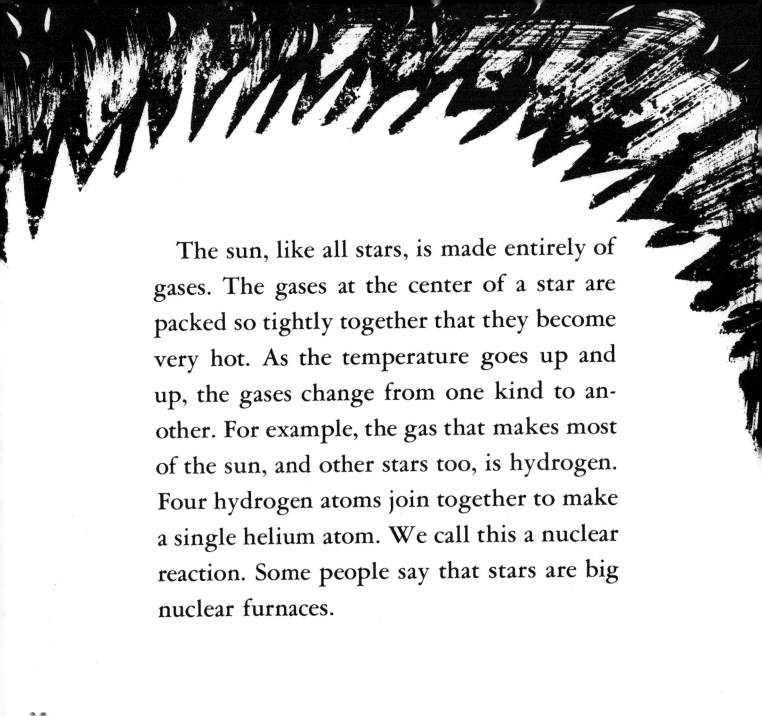

The sun, like all stars, is made entirely of gases. The gases at the center of a star are packed so tightly together that they become very hot. As the temperature goes up and up, the gases change from one kind to another. For example, the gas that makes most of the sun, and other stars too, is hydrogen. Four hydrogen atoms join together to make a single helium atom. We call this a nuclear reaction. Some people say that stars are big nuclear furnaces.

Certain stars produce much more heat, light, and other forms of energy than other stars. There are hot stars and cool ones. There are bright stars and dim ones. The bright ones are usually hot stars. But not always. A small hot star may be dimmer than a large cool star.

Stars seem to remain motionless in space. As long as we look at the stars in the Big Dipper, for example, they will be in the same position where we now see them. As long as men have been observing the stars, their positions have not changed. Therefore many people think no changes ever take place. But stars move in many ways.

Most stars rotate; that is, they spin around just as the earth does. The sun takes about twenty-six days to spin around once. Some stars rotate faster than the sun, some rotate more slowly. Perhaps there are others that do not rotate at all, but astronomers believe this is most unlikely.

THE SUN MOVES TWELVE MILES A SECOND

EARTH

Besides rotating, stars also move through space. The sun moves about twelve miles a second toward the constellation Hercules. And it carries the whole solar system with it, including the earth.

Because stars are so far away, we are not aware of their motions. If you stood on the curb and a car passed by you at sixty miles an hour, you would know the car was moving because it would be close to you.

But if the car were two or three miles away from you, you would not notice the motion nearly as much. That's the way it is with stars. Stars move very fast, but we are not aware of their motions because the stars are so far away.

The drawing shows the stars of the Big Dipper. Astronomers know the speed and the direction of each star in the Dipper. The arrows show the way the stars are moving. The longer the arrow, the faster the speed of the star.

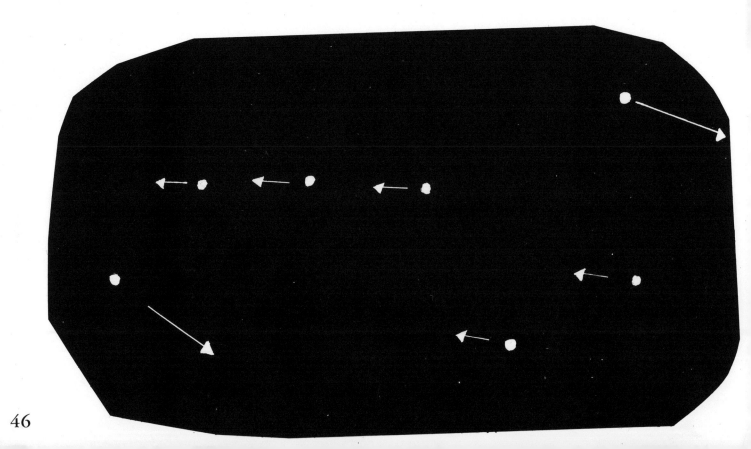

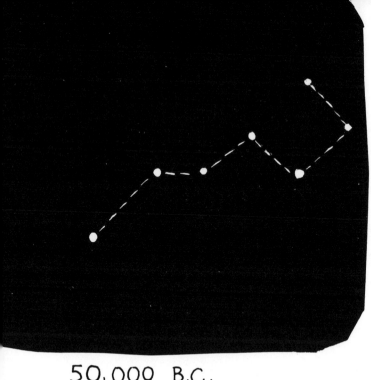

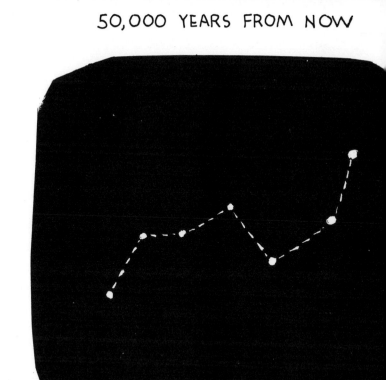

50,000 B.C.

Long ago the Big Dipper looked different from the way it looks now. Fifty thousand years from now it will look different from the way it looks today.

47

Stars move. But because our lifetimes are so short, you and I can notice no change in the positions of the stars.

Where do stars come from and what happens to them?

Stars do not last forever. Astronomers believe that stars blow up, and the gases that made them spread out into space.

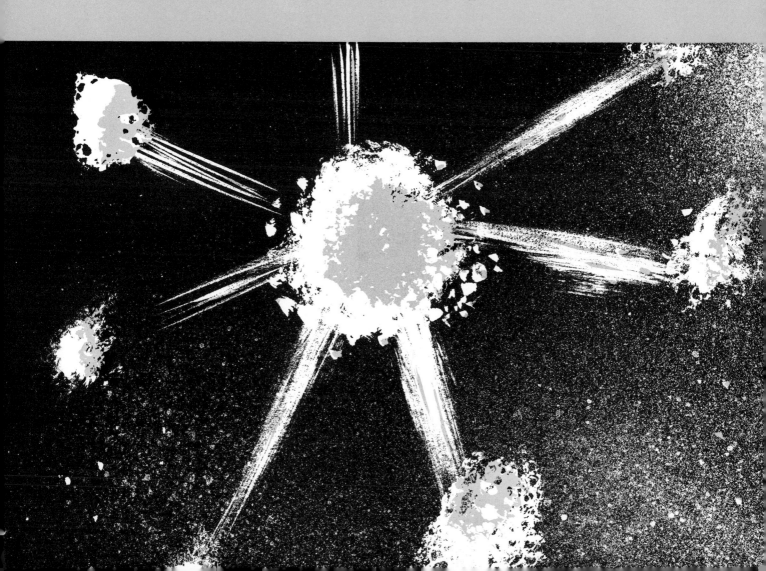

After a long time, millions and billions of years, gases in space gather together. These gases come from stars that have exploded, and they also come from space between the stars. Space is not empty. In every part of our own galaxy each cubic inch of space contains sixteen atoms of hydrogen gas. Every cubic mile of so-called empty space contains about one hundred dust particles. That's not very much material. But space is vast and so the total amount of hydrogen and dust in space is very great. There's more than enough hydrogen to make multitudes of stars.

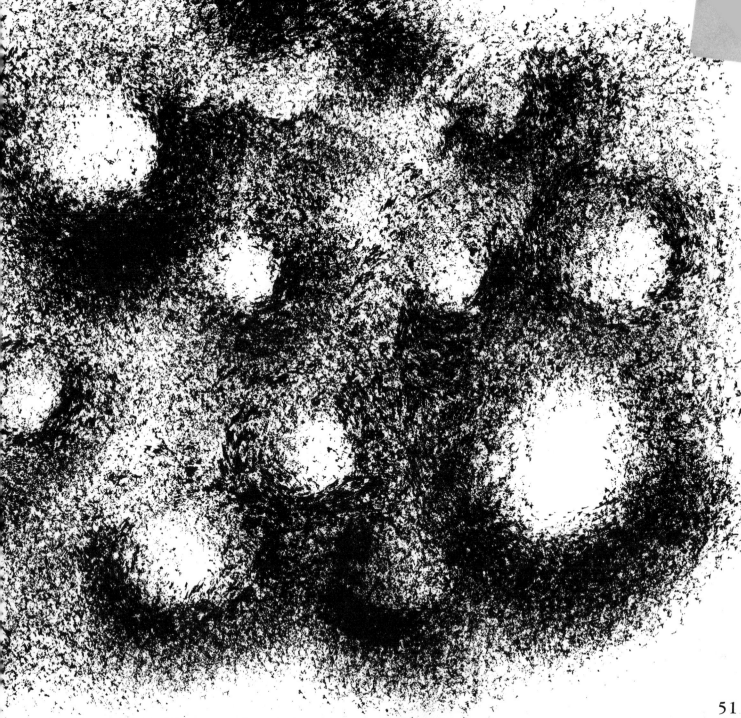

51

In many locations in our galaxy, great
quantities of gases have collected together.
These collections are called nebulas.

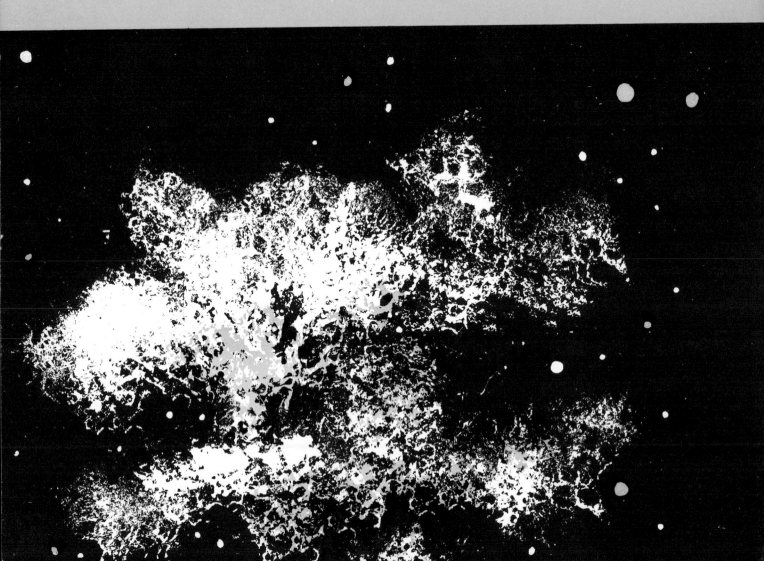

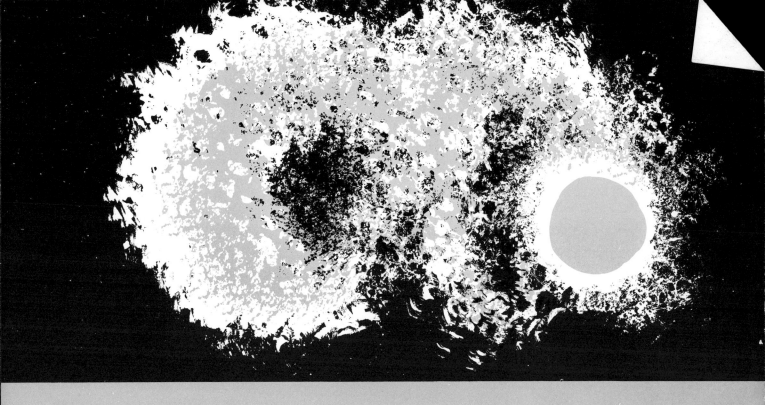

Astronomers often see dark specks in some of these nebulas. They believe specks are places where gases are packed tightly together. More and more gases collect, and they become hotter and hotter. After hundreds of thousands of years, the gases are so hot that nuclear reactions begin. A new star is created.

If the amount of matter in the new star is small, the star will be a feeble, dim object. If there is a large amount of material in the star, it will be hot and bright. After billions of years the star will cool. It may blow up. Once again gases are set free in space, gases that may become part of another new star.

In your lifetime, you will probably see no changes in the appearance of the stars, no changes in their positions. But during your lifetime, as always, new stars are being created. Bright stars are becoming dimmer. Old stars, once bright and clear, are changing into black dwarfs. And all the stars in this galaxy of ours are traveling their separate ways, as indeed are all the stars in all the galaxies that make the universe.

ABOUT THE AUTHOR

Dr. Franklyn M. Branley is well known as the author of many excellent science books for young people of all ages. He is also co-editor of the Let's-Read-and-Find-Out Science Books.

Dr. Branley is Astronomer and Assistant Chairman of the American Museum-Hayden Planetarium in New York City. He is Director of Educational Services for the Planetarium, where popular courses in astronomy, navigation, and meteorology are given for people of all ages. He is interested in all phases of astronomy and the national space program, and he teaches young people, adults, and teachers in these subjects.

Dr. Branley holds degrees from New York University, Columbia University, and from the New York State University College at New Paltz. He lives with his family in Woodcliff Lake, New Jersey.

ABOUT THE ILLUSTRATOR

Leonard Kessler is a writer and illustrator of children's books as well as a designer and commercial artist. He became interested in children's books as a result of teaching art to young people in summer camps.

Mr. Kessler was born in Akron, Ohio, but he moved east to Pittsburgh at an early age. He was graduated from the Carnegie Institute of Technology with a degree in fine arts, painting, and design. Mr. Kessler enjoys playing the clarinet in his leisure time. He lives in New City, New York.